Wild cky A...als!

"Hiya, I'm Zeek."

"Hi, I'm Finn."

Calling all aliens!

Are you planning a holiday to planet Earth?

Finn and Zeek are here to help.

'Wild and Wacky Animals'
Published by MAVERICK ARTS PUBLISHING LTD
Studio 3A, City Business Centre, 6 Brighton Road,
Horsham, West Sussex, RH13 5BB, +44 (0)1403 256941
© Maverick Arts Publishing Limited May 2019

A CIP catalogue record for this book is available at the British Library.

ISBN 978-1-84886-465-8

Maverick publishing
www.maverickbooks.co.uk

Credits:
Finn & Zeek illustrations by Jake McDonald, Bright Illustration Agency
Cover: Jake McDonald/Bright, Jane Burton /naturepl.com
Inside: **Naturepl.com:** Gerrit Vyn (6), Luiz Claudio Marigo (8), MYN / Lily Kumpe (9), MYN / Marc Pihet (9), Alex Hyde (9), Brent Stephenson (10), Onne van der Wal (11), Mark Payne-Gill (12), Rolf Nussbaumer (13), Konrad Wothe (14), Flip de Nooyer /Minden (15), Magnus Lungren / Wild Wonders of China (16), Kerstin Hinze (17), Ken Preston-Mafham / PREMAPHOTOS (17), Edwin Giesbers (18), Bernard Castelein (18), Mary McDonald (19), David Shale (20), Denis-Huot (22 & 23), Colin Seddon (22), Aflo (23), Dave Watts (24), D. Parer & E.Parer-Cook/ Minden (25), Markus Varesvuo (25), Dietmar Nill (25), Edwin Giesbers (25), Jane Burton (27)

This book is rated as: Purple Band (Guided Reading)

Wild and Wacky Animals

Contents

Introduction	4
Staying Alive	8
Stick Insect	8
Flying Fish	10
Puffer Fish	11
Amazing Armour	12
Wacky and Whiffy	14
Stink Birds	14
Sea Hares	16
Millipedes	17
Luring Looks	18
Peafowl	18
Anglerfish	20
Mammal Mix Up	22
Okapi	22
Platypus	24
Quiz	28
Index/Glossary	30

INCOMING MESSAGE

Dear Finn and Zeek,

We want to visit Earth, but we're worried about some of the weird creatures on it!

Please can you show us some of the wackiest animals so that we are prepared?

From
Bim and Bam
(Planet Bland)

Over a very long time, animals have changed to help them live in their **environments**. This means there are some very wacky looking animals out there!

Flamingos have long necks and legs so they can go into deeper water to get food.

Also, flamingos are pink due to the algae and shrimp they eat!

Staying Alive! Stick Insect

Some animals look like things around them to escape being eaten. The stick insect looks like a stick! No animal wants to eat a stick!

They are usually green or brown but some can be more colourful.

Stick insects mostly come out at night and eat leaves.

Staying Alive! Flying Fish

Fish are best known for swimming but these flying fish can also fly! They have wing-like fins to help them take off. This means that they can fly out of the water, away from any sneaky **predators**.

Fins

Is it a bird? Is it a plane? Nope, it's a fish!

Pufferfish

Before

Pufferfish are very slow and clumsy swimmers. They puff up to make it difficult for **predators** to get them.

After

Staying Alive! Amazing Armour

Some animals have very tough skin to protect them. The armadillo is covered in bony plates and has skin like leather. This armour is so tough, it means **predators** can't hurt it. Its name means 'little armoured one' in Spanish.

Some armadillos can even curl into a ball to avoid **predators**.

13

Wacky and Whiffy! Hoatzin Bird

The hoatzin bird is not just wacky because of its punk hairdo, it also smells… really bad. Their nickname is 'Stink Birds'! The hoatzin bird smells like cow poop because of the plants they eat.

Pooey!

Although they don't do this on purpose, it means nothing even wants to come near them!

Hoatzin chicks are born with claws on their wings, like dinosaurs! Weird!

Wacky and Whiffy! Sea Hares

A sea hare's skin is covered in a **toxin** that makes them taste very bad. They can also let off an ink which smells horrible to other animals. Both these things stop **predators** from eating them!

Millipedes

They smell even worse than my socks!

Although millipedes have lots of legs, they are quite slow! To protect themselves they let off a bad smell.

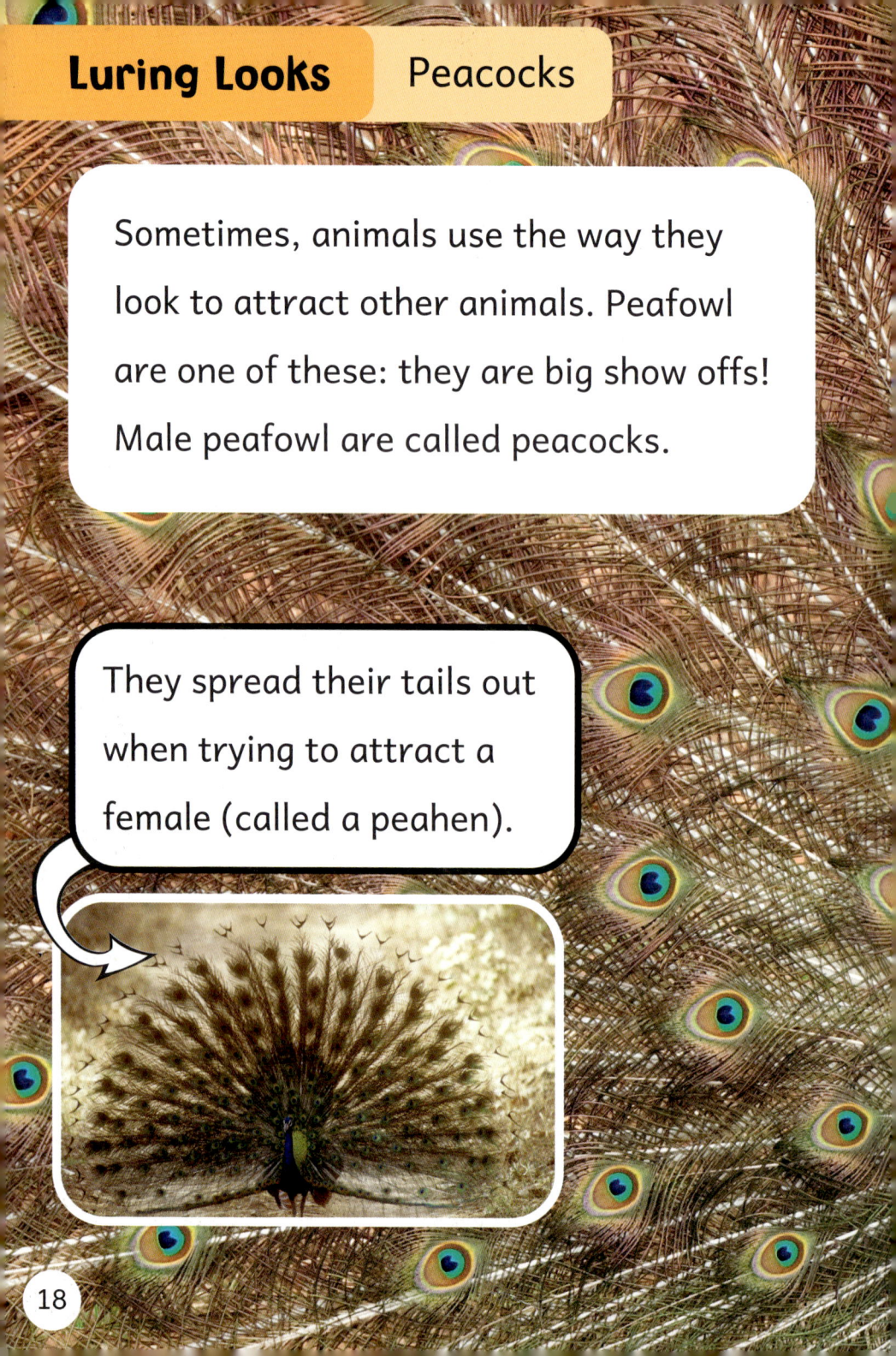

Luring Looks — Peacocks

Sometimes, animals use the way they look to attract other animals. Peafowl are one of these: they are big show offs! Male peafowl are called peacocks.

They spread their tails out when trying to attract a female (called a peahen).

They have amazing, long tail feathers.

Luring Looks   Angler Fish

The angler fish is anything but beautiful! It lives very deep in the sea, where it is completely dark.

The female angler fish has a long pole coming from her head. This pole has a light on the end, which attracts **prey**. Their mouths are so big they can swallow something double their size.

Mammal Mix Up! Okapi

Some animals seem to look like a weird mix of other animals. This is so it can be well suited to where it lives.

Okapis are a bit like giraffes, and a bit like zebras. They live in the **rainforest**. They have a long blue tongues so they can reach high leaves, like a giraffe. They also have stripy legs like a zebra to blend into their surroundings.

Okapi

Giraffe

Okapi

Zebra

Mammal Mix Up! Platypus

The platypus is one of two **mammals** that lay eggs!

Like the okapi, the platypus looks like a mix of other creatures to fit into its environment.

The platypus has a bill and webbed feet, like a duck.

It has a tail like a beaver.

Its body and fur are like an otter.

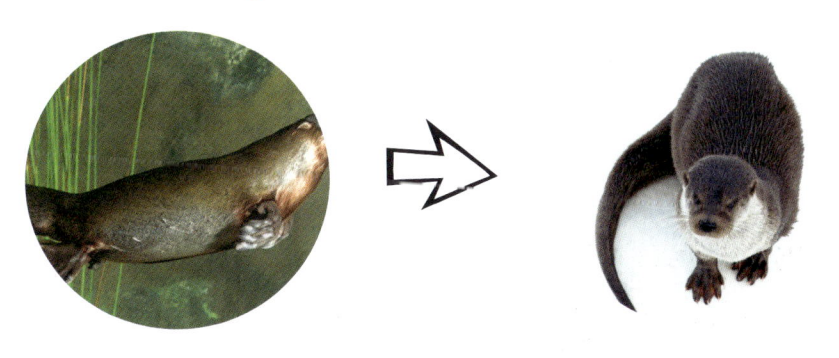

25

MESSAGE SENT

Dear Bim and Bam,

Animals on planet Earth are very wacky! But in most cases they are wacky for a reason. Lots of them are just trying to avoid predators, so they won't bother you!

If you are visiting Mexico, perhaps go and see this happy little creature called an axolotl.

From,
Finn and Zeek x

Axolotl from Mexico

Quiz

1. What do stick insects eat?
a) Leaves
b) Sticks
c) Fish

2. What does armadillo mean in Spanish?
a) Armoured roller
b) One with armour
c) Little armoured one

3. What is a female peafowl called?
a) Peacock
b) Peagirl
c) Peahen

4. Where do angler fish live?
a) In the deep, dark sea
b) In the top, light sea
c) In the dark underground

5. What colour is the okapi's tongue?
a) Yellow
b) Blue
c) Pink

5. The platypus is one of only two mammals that...
a) Has fur
b) Swims
c) Lays eggs

Index/Glossary

Environments pg 6
Everything that surrounds a living thing.

Mammal pg 24
Warm-blooded animals with hair or fur. They feed milk to their young. Humans are mammals.

Predator pg 10, 11, 12, 16
An animal that hunts other animals (prey).

Prey pg 21
An animal that is hunted by another animal.

Rainforest pg 22
A woodland with tall, evergreen trees. It rains a lot in a rainforest.

Toxin pg 16
A substance created by something living, which is dangerous to other living things.

Word Break Down

Quiz Answers:

1. a, 2. c, 3. c, 4. a, 5. b, 6. c

Environments
En-vi-ron-ments

Predators
Pred-a-tors

Armoured
Ar-mour-ed

Hoatzin
Hoh-at-sin

Millipedes
Mil-le-pede

Okapi
Oh-kah-pee

Axolotl
Ak-suh-lot-l

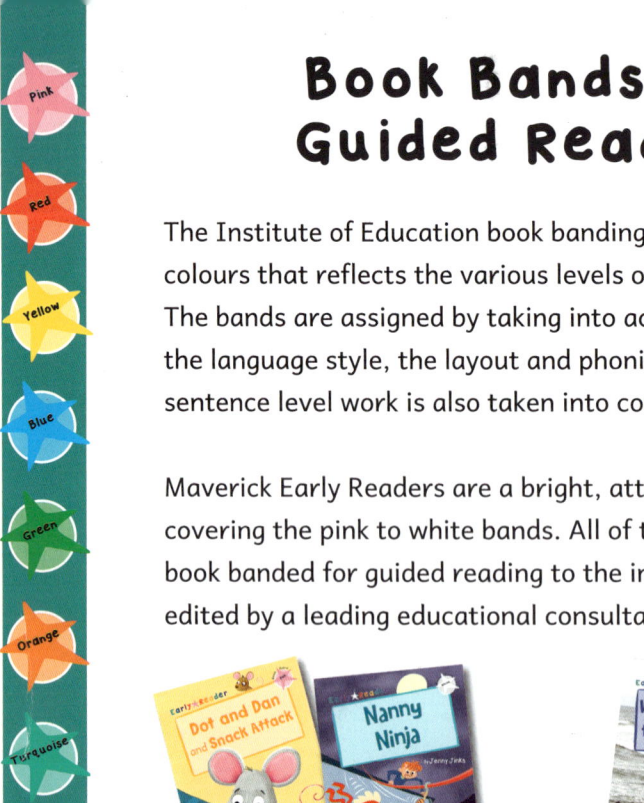

Book Bands for Guided Reading

The Institute of Education book banding system is a scale of colours that reflects the various levels of reading difficulty. The bands are assigned by taking into account the content, the language style, the layout and phonics. Word, phrase and sentence level work is also taken into consideration.

Maverick Early Readers are a bright, attractive range of books covering the pink to white bands. All of these books have been book banded for guided reading to the industry standard and edited by a leading educational consultant.

Fiction

Non-fiction

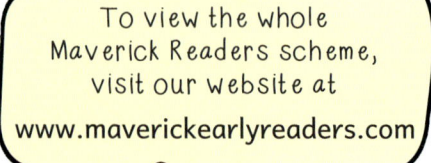

To view the whole Maverick Readers scheme, visit our website at www.maverickearlyreaders.com

Or scan the QR code above to view our scheme instantly!